This book belongs to:

....

....

PASTEL GOTH CHIBI GIRL KAWAII AND CREEPY COLORING BOOK

Pastel Goth Chibi Girl Kawaii And Creepy Coloring Book help your child be creative with the same colors and drawings with cute and funny pictures. Practice the dexterity of the hands and how to appraise the delicate color of the brain. Help improve the ability to think images, colors, concentration and your child form a clear, vivid worldview. The book with a nice eye design, a graphic image would have brought you the interest.

Deidre Motys is a publisher of fun and relaxing coloring books for kids and adults. Be sure to check out other unique and creative titles.

Happy Coloring!

PASTEL GOTH CHIBI GIRL KAWAII AND CREEPY COLORING BOOK

PASTEL GOTH CHIBI GIRL KAWAII AND
CREEPY COLORING BOOK

RiP
RiP
RiP

PASTEL GOTH CHIBI GIRL KAWAII AND
CREEPY COLORING BOOK

PASTEL GOTH CHIBI GIRL KAWAII AND
CREEPY COLORING BOOK

PASTEL GOTH CHIBI GIRL KAWAII AND CREEPY COLORING BOOK

Boo!

PASTEL GOTH CHIBI GIRL KAWAII AND
CREEPY COLORING BOOK

PASTEL GOTH CHIBI GIRL KAWAII AND
CREEPY COLORING BOOK

PASTEL GOTH CHIBI GIRL KAWAII AND
CREEPY COLORING BOOK

PASTEL GOTH CHIBI GIRL KAWAII AND
CREEPY COLORING BOOK

PASTEL GOTH CHIBI GIRL KAWAII AND
CREEPY COLORING BOOK

PASTEL GOTH CHIBI GIRL KAWAII AND
CREEPY COLORING BOOK

R.I.P
R.I.P

PASTEL GOTH CHIBI GIRL KAWAII AND
CREEPY COLORING BOOK

BLOOD
10
6

PASTEL GOTH CHIBI GIRL KAWAII AND
CREEPY COLORING BOOK

PASTEL GOTH CHIBI GIRL KAWAII AND
CREEPY COLORING BOOK

PASTEL GOTH CHIBI GIRL KAWAII AND
CREEPY COLORING BOOK

PASTEL GOTH CHIBI GIRL KAWAII AND
CREEPY COLORING BOOK

PASTEL GOTH CHIBI GIRL KAWAII AND
CREEPY COLORING BOOK

PASTEL GOTH CHIBI GIRL KAWAII AND
CREEPY COLORING BOOK

PASTEL GOTH CHIBI GIRL KAWAII AND
CREEPY COLORING BOOK

PASTEL GOTH CHIBI GIRL KAWAII AND
CREEPY COLORING BOOK

PASTEL GOTH CHIBI GIRL KAWAII AND
CREEPY COLORING BOOK

PASTEL GOTH CHIBI GIRL KAWAII AND
CREEPY COLORING BOOK

PASTEL GOTH CHIBI GIRL KAWAII AND
CREEPY COLORING BOOK

PASTEL GOTH CHIBI GIRL KAWAII AND
CREEPY COLORING BOOK

PASTEL GOTH CHIBI GIRL KAWAII AND
CREEPY COLORING BOOK

PASTEL GOTH CHIBI GIRL KAWAII AND
CREEPY COLORING BOOK

PASTEL GOTH CHIBI GIRL KAWAII AND
CREEPY COLORING BOOK

PASTEL GOTH CHIBI GIRL KAWAII AND
CREEPY COLORING BOOK